At The Core of Me

Parminder Syan

At The Core of Me © 2023 Parminder Syan

All rights reserved.

No part of this publication may be reproduced, stored in a retrieval system, or transmitted, in any form or by any means, electronic, mechanical, photocopying, recording, or otherwise, without the prior written permission of the presenters.

Parminder Syan asserts the moral right to be identified as the author of this work.

Presentation by *BookLeaf Publishing*

Web: www.bookleafpub.com

E-mail: info@bookleafpub.com

ISBN: 9789357744164

First edition 2023

I would like to dedicate my debut solo poetry book to all of the friends and family that remain in my life. Thank you all for your support, encouragement and appreciation for my hard work. Thank you also, to the many poets who have supported me from the beginning on my social media platforms.

Kiran and Amy, my beautiful daughters, thank you for being you. I know that you will be proud of me. Love you both with all my heart.

Raj Rani. Thank you for EVERYTHING..

Bal, my dearest lifelong friend of over 35 years, you kept saying "Write a book" Here you go, I did it!

Amyah and A.J. I leave this and future books as a legacy to you both.

Love you for eternity. Nunni x

ACKNOWLEDGEMENT

First and foremost, I would like to thank God and the Universe for bringing me this opportunity. I am humbly grateful.

This may seem conceited, but I have to acknowledge my own strength, for not giving up and fighting on a daily basis to remain sane all the while, bleeding ink onto paper, it may just as well have been my blood. I created over one hundred poems and survived to tell the tale.

Finally, a huge thank you to BookLeaf Publishing for this brilliant initiative, to encourage novice writers, like myself, to take the leap.

PREFACE

I studied Counseling Skills in 2019, yet nothing could prepare me for this phase of my life.

I learned more through this transitional phase, which gave me the tools to manage my own mental health.

I write this book from my own personal experiences, in the knowledge that it will help readers to understand that they are not alone, during their own journey, towards discovering their true Self.

Deterioration of the mental and physical aspects of us, are all part of the process. The thoughts and emotions can be overwhelming and incredibly intense.

At The Core of Me

At the core of me lies the biggest heart
Filled with love, hope and divinity.
Not just for this world, but for all of Infinity.
Never stopping to think for my own gain
Continuing to shower endless love, despite all my pain
Still barely intact, after having pieced myself back together
Ruptured, broken, and shattered, wickedly without thought
Like shards of glistening glass, re-kindled in the hearth
Made whole again with the heat and re-tethered
At the core of me lies this beautiful soul
Who chose to tread the most difficult of life's journey
That of a mother, a warrior, a queen, and a woman of God
To show others the light, is my sacred destiny
At the core of me, is my sheer glorious essence
Humbly mindful and fully aware of my own presence
A tool for the Almighty to utilize me for His work

To leave behind a legacy of love when I leave this world
At the core of me you will find a plethora of gargantuan emotions
Never yet had I felt, until this moment in my life
A magnanimous list, too difficult to write without emotion
To pen such an illustrious listing
Will consume the rest of my life
Ultimately until. My last dying breath.

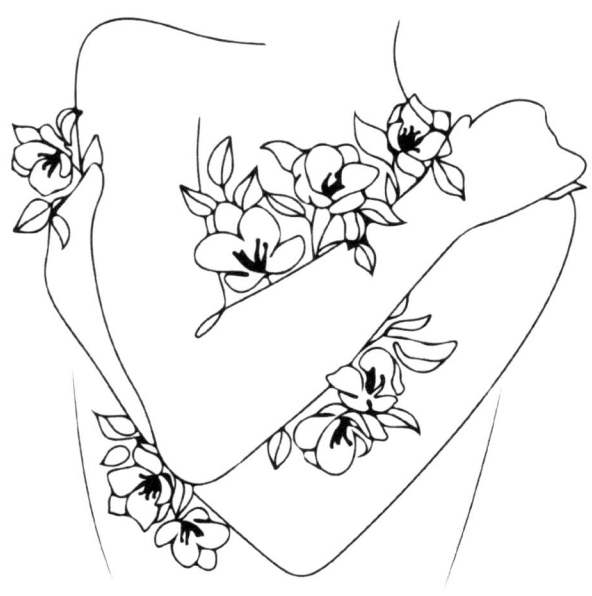

Magic Weaver

I weave magic with twenty-six letters
Creating a page full of words
Intricately forming to convey
The true heart of the matter
God, love, mental health, life and despair
Hoping that it will aid,
Someone else, to heal and repair
Matters, of their own heart
I do not know, if what I write
Is actually poetry, because
I have no real comprehension
Regarding styles or formations
Yet, every single poem I compile
Satisfies me with an internal peace
Emanating a huge smile
Within my whole being
Once again, I have expelled
Everything inside of me
Out into the vastness of the Universe
Setting my burdened soul free
My feelings, I have vomited into space
Beyond the Milky Way, my verses transcend
Echoing back to Earth, with a silent bang
Into the brains of foes and friends
Hoping that they may be able to comprehend

Exactly what I had conjured, in my head
Whilst weaving magic with twenty-six letters
Casting an everlasting poetical spell.

A Bad Day

The heart, it is beating,
Yet, not feeling anything
The body keeps moving
On autopilot, intuitively
The internal organs
Functioning at their best
Fighting another grueling bout
Fatigue, depression, anxiety and stress
How can one be of any use
If only, for just one's self?
The dark clouds are here again
Despite the glorious sunshine
Wishing that they would disappear
Unable, not wanting to tolerate
Any more of this unbearable pain
Standing under the running water
Showering, before trying to sleep
Pulling down the skin on her face
Stopping the tears from forming
Scratching her body with her nails
Wanting to dig deeper, until she bleeds
In the hope of eradicating all her sadness
As her blood pours down the drain
Washing away the internal demons
In hope of drowning her endless pain.

Void Of Feelings

There are days when I am void
Numb, to every feeling
Admittedly, I can feel my heart
In my chest, still beating
Pushing the blood around my being
Keeping me alive, functioning
My brain is on overload today
To the point, that I want to end it all
I am trying so hard
Not to think, too much
About anything at all
On days like this, being alive
Is just too overwhelming
To take back control
I know what I must do
Sit down, take deep breaths
Slow my heart rate down
My mind will follow soon
I hate it when this happens
Life spiraling out of control
Heavy with anxiety-fuelled breathes
I hurry myself to get dressed
Urgently, as I quicken my pace
I become even more distressed
Agitated, desperate to escape

Not thinking clearly,
Leaving the house, totally oblivious
I find myself, at the park
Bathing with light from the sun now
My demeanor, no longer dark
I post comical Instagram stories
Applying funny filters, as my mask
To hide my true feelings, from the world
In the hope of giving them a laugh
These summer walks, lift my spirit
Making me forget all my troubles
I watch happy families, playing together
It is beautiful that they have one another
To help get through each day together.

Feeling Lost

You were asking today; How did I feel?
My tears I could not hold.
I pushed them back hard, as so not to reveal
The hidden story of my battered soul
My quivering voice begins to break
"I am okay" To you I say
"I know you too well," you replied
You are not yourself today
Why do you really feel like this
What is bothering you today?"
You continued gently, to question me
In your own concerned way
"I feel that I am going nowhere
Not just because of lockdown
I no longer feel a part of this world
My mind is no longer my own
I feel like, I have been lost in translation
Involuntarily, pushed through revolving doors
I am lost in a rapidly changing world
Every minute, I feel increasingly unsure
I do not know, what I want anymore
The language of today, has changed so much
During these dreadful Covid times
Social distancing, lockdown, wear a mask
I need to know, when will it all end?

I come from a different world.
Where there was no social media
Now everyday people have the power
To stir up mass hysteria
So many changes I have seen
I cannot keep up, alas it seems
Not just in the world today, itself
That also too, deeply within myself
The changes they are like growing pains
Crushing and unwanted, yet oh so necessary
Molding me into becoming, another's adversary
To aid them on this journey, of life's train
I must transform and shed my old skin
Ultimately, to be comfortable again
I have forgotten how it feels to be happy
This whole transition within, evokes so much pain
This old version of me, I have to let her go
To allow the light back in to shine
In 54 years, for the very first time
Every second, of every day, is only mine
Learning to let go of all my fears
Guided, unknowingly by The Divine.

Buried

I buried myself, so deep within me
Thus, I lost myself completely
Curled up like a fetus, sinking in my misery
Secretly, I reveled in the turmoil
Buried, away from the eyes of the world
I convinced myself that this was
The only way, to survive it all
To become invisible and unheard
Each time I reached above my head
To break through the muddy soil
My soul fearfully, cringed and recoiled
Comparable to an Olympic swimmer
Competing against his own best time
Fiercely fighting the strongest of currents
In the deepest, depths of his own mind
Yet, just still barely treading the waters
I too have been mercilessly, beaten aback
Despite my own strong willpower
The constant self-judgment of my own
self-awareness,
To do good, in the eyes of God above
Yet somehow, I still epically failed
Managing to hurt the people that I love
Unintentionally, of course
I am only human, after all

This does not mean, that I am a bad person
Or that I have a dark heart or soul
It just means, that I have sown
The seeds of my own karma
Debts to repay as they unfold
Here on Earth, before I go
God, forbid I have to come back
I vehemently refuse to, it is too damn hard
Exhausted and tearful, I told my friend
"I do not owe my children anything
I will leave them enough money to pay
For my funeral and farewell prayers
Including that last piece of clothing,
Covering my body, on my final journey
Happy finally, to meet my beloved Maker
The one and only, to judge me."

Let me Sleep

Arousing from my sleep, abruptly I awoke
Startled by the rude interruption,
Heralded by the morning, as it broke
Piercing the peace and quiet
Of the blissful realm of darkness
Not yet wanting, to wake up at all
Forcing tightly, my eyelids I closed
The rising dawn, beckons me
To accept another day, as it unfolds
Subjecting me to feel everything
Right down to the earth's core
Thus, I want to remain asleep
I do not want to open my eyes
My impatient soul informs me
That it is time to start the day
Whether I want to, or not
Mechanically, performing daily actions
Mindlessly, like a programmed robot
Operating only on half-full batteries
My heart not feeling anything at all
I am failing, to convey the jumble
That is in my frazzled head
Because, you would have needed
To have walked, in my shoes instead
To fully grasp the enormity of my plight

Or even begin to remotely understand
Why all I want to do right now, is sleep
Wallowing in my bed, in a folded heap
My intention is, not to be morbid
I know I have so much life, left to live
After all, today was not a bad day
It was just one, of many days
That I was finding it difficult to live.

Pieces

I do not recognize, the person that I have
become, let's say
Once again I am lost, somewhere in translation
People came and took pieces of me
Along the bloody way
Some are still doing this today
I guess I am still on my path
To becoming someone else
A different version of my former self
I don't quite know what more to say
Except that I know I will get there one day
Uncertain of where my destination lies
Other than Heaven, eventually, that is
But what is my path in-between
I guess I must keep moving forward
Until my ordained death arrives
Only then, peace will be bestowed upon me.

Last Laugh

I want to take a sharp-edged razor
To cut out the voices in my head
The ones that are stopping me
Living my life, as I try to move ahead
The demons sent to me
By my non well-wishing enemies
Endeavoring to stop my progression
In fulfilling my own prophecy
How fearful they must be of me
To stoop to such lowly actions
In cahoots, with Satan himself
Lest they forget, inevitably
Everything has an equal
And opposite reaction
They keep trying to beat me
But I refuse to be beaten
By them or any other unworldly entity
I am me, a child of God
Don't forget, that will be your humiliation
Light will always prevail over the dark
That is how He works His Creation
Keep watching, I promise you
I will have the last laugh.

I Am Done

Standing by the window, I had a deja vu
I do not want to live this life, anymore
Last lifetime, I did not make it through
Hence, I have landed back here again
How much more pain must I tolerate?
Constantly being in merciless limbo
I remain stuck firmly at the crossroads
I do not even want to have to choose
Which way I need or have to go!
I give up, trying so damn hard
To get through each day
My best is just not good enough
My ageing body is giving up on me
Dashing hopes of living a fuller life
If I cannot fend for myself
How am I supposed to survive?
All on my own, me, myself, and I
Am I cursed to still live?
How many more years before I die?
I have had enough. Exasperated
I just want out of here
I have given all of me, done my darndest
With nothing left to give to anyone
The time is right for me to finally rest
It is time to leave, I am done!

I Want to Go Home

I was having one of those, anxiety-filled days again,
My mind in such turmoil, that I am unable to think straight
I have been housebound for days, due to the ceaseless rain
Dreadful days of stormy weather, are forcing me to refrain
From taking my daily walk, to free the maddening thoughts in my brain
The skies are full of crashing thunder, making me jump out of my skin
Loudly like a horses whip, lightning cracks across the skies
Akin to a scene from a horror film, before someone is about to die
Grey bulging clouds move cumbersomely, heavy with rain ensue
Stopping and starting, with brighter sunny intervals in-between skies so blue
Thus conjuring magical, unicorn-coloured rainbows on the horizon
The rain continues to howl, swirling around the top of the house

Battering all walls of my extended room,
perched high on its own

My thoughts already a jumbled mess, ran even further astray
"The winds were going to rip my room off, from the rest of the house today!
That would not be such a terrible thing, in fact, then I could escape this world."
I wished hard for the treacherous winds, to blow me far away
Casting me with my inner turbulent storm, into the eye of the storm on display
I am not looking for any of this, to make any sense at all, in any way
Suddenly, I envision myself wearing the sparkling *Red Ruby Slippers
Belonging to *Dorothy from the *Wizard of Oz with her dog *Toto
Praying I too, could close my eyes, excitedly click my heels, as she did
To truly find my way, to my new home, a peaceful place in my head
Without landing on a *Wicked Witch, who was unexpectedly dead!

*Referenced "The Wizard of Oz"
By L. Frank Baum

Inside Outside

She stares at the reflection in the mirror
Deeply into the pools of her sad, brown eyes
Desperately searching, to find her happy place
Lost somewhere within herself, deep inside
Happy momentarily, because has fixed the outside
Indulging herself in a brand-new hairstyle
Laced with autumnal brown and ginger hues
In the hope of lifting the darkness
Within her mind, that she is so afraid to lose
She has adorned her face heavily
Painting it with brand new makeup, she treated herself to
A prominent, blood-red lipstick, emblazons her lips
To chase away her ongoing blues
Deep down, she knows, it is herself she is trying to mask
Showing people that she is well; in case they should ask
A new application of gel nails too
Hours spent pampering her lithe brown fingers
Coloured to match her new hair, a gorgeous deep ginger

She is trying her hardest every day, to find her inner peace
Beautifying herself externally, with these acts
Fully aware, that it is all just a temporary fix
Right now, in this moment, it is what she desperately needs
These are her only tricks, to avoid the insanity
A clever distraction not to look internally
Validating herself, in the here and now
Not knowing what tomorrow will bring
Tirelessly she continues to fulfill, these small steps of self-love
Desperately remaining hopeful, in the knowledge that one day
Her mind, body and soul, will become entirely whole again.

A Better Day

Today I feel so happy, at the park
Sitting on this worn-out bench
On this glorious sunny day
My mind, not sitting in the dark
Today is a good day in my head
I feel light and I have energy
I am grateful I could leave my bed
To be in complete synergy
With my beautiful self
Today I want to do many things
Hence, I tidied up the mess in my room.
Out came the yellow cleaning cloths
Detergents, mop and the broom
I thought about what I wanted to eat for dinner
What shall I cook for myself?
Today I want to speak with people
Have deep and meaningful conversations
Today I want to do so much!
Without hindrance or hesitation
In this present moment, basking in the sunshine
I realize that what is meant for me
Shall be mine
I live in God's heart, as He does mine
Truly, I feel humbled, blessed by the Divine
Tomorrow is another day

I do not know what it will hold
Will I even want to leave my bed?
Will it be dark or light in my head?
Thus, I take each day, one at a time
Taking nothing for granted
Quietly confident in knowing, eventually everything will be okay
I will have everything I have ever wanted
Just stuck a little in my head right now
I know it will not last forever
So much is left to learn, to grow
Today is such a good day!
I must continue to endeavor.

Emotional Clouds

Today, the silent swirling clouds
Roaming the opulent October skies
Emulate my tumultuous emotions
So deeply being felt, today
Partly full of questionable tears
Yet no desire to shed
In the vastness of it all
Will any of it really matter
To anyone, except me, that I know?
It is all inside of my head, in my DNA
That no one else, can ever console
But the clouds relate to my sorrow
Unanimously agreeable and fully attuned
With the recesses of my heart and soul.

Emptied By Life

A vast feeling of emptiness within
Life has sucked her completely dry
Selflessly giving out her heart and soul
She caused her own untimely demise
Emptying herself of everything she had
Lost and confused, no longer knowing
How to give back to her own self
Her aspiring dreams and hopes dashed
Thanks to unexpected failing health
Dissociated completely from this world
No desire of wanting to belong
Fearful of stepping out of the door
Everything appears to be alien to her
It is excruciating for her broken soul
Trapped unequivocally, with no hope of escape
Sad and alone, on this earth, called home
Allegedly, so many friends and family
Yet not one solitary person did ask
Never did she contemplate
Even in her wildest dreams
That life could ever be this incomplete
Gathering her thoughts, coming back to self
Her breathing returning to its normal pace
"It's okay," she comforts herself
"You are exactly where you are meant to be."

Way Back Home

I went to give a blood sample today
To make sure that I am still human
(After making friends with Covid twice)
I wonder, am I in hell or heaven?
It was in a tall, modern glass building
Located near the train station
On a whim afterwards
I jumped onto the DLR train
(I forgot where my spaceship was)
Long Covid has got my brain confuddled,
I really cannot remember, f*ck all at times
My head has been, well and truly scuppered
I do thank God however
That it's not totally f*ckered
Otherwise, I would not have remembered
Which train I need to take, to go back home
Never mind, if I cannot find my spaceship
I will just wait until such time
To be located by my alien friends, so I may return back home.

Somewhere In Between

Most days I sit here alone,
Yet, I no longer feel lonely.
Ascension is a beautiful journey
Transcending to your very bones
You no longer desire to tolerate
To argue, disagree or berate
Every feeling, that no longer holds place
In your vessel, now full of grace
Your heart and mind are finally at peace
Is this how heaven on earth is supposed to feel?
That is not to say, that there are no dark days
They always manage to worm their way
Back to the darkest corners of my mind
Reminding me of all my painful days, left behind
On days that I do not want to leave my bed
I force myself, exhausted, to still function,
Frustrated with all the nonsense
I shout out loudly, to myself, and my silly head
"Please, today, I do not want to malfunction."

Ascension Chronicles

So many turbulent thoughts and feelings churning inside of me
Not knowing whether I am coming or going
The harder I try to rationalize my mind, or sort myself out
The deeper and deeper, I find myself reeling
No one ever taught me, how to manage my mind
My finances, relationships, or my damn life
I learnt on the job, falling and stumbling, bruising along the way
Not knowing that I would have to travel
To the deepest and darkest, recesses of myself
Where I drown daily, realizing that, only I can save myself
By navigating the depths of my soul, to haul myself out of that hell
To master and execute such a feat, is not always possible for everyone
So many of us, do not ever make it back, giving in to death
We fail the road to Ascension, that the Universe sent us to test
Unable to grasp or fathom, how to take back control of our mind

We lose the battle, by giving up and taking away our own life
To sleep permanently, is the only solution that we can see at the time
Thinking that it is only death, that will put an end to our daily strife.

Not Listening

Today I refuse to listen to them
The infernal voices in my head
Screaming silently, yet loud enough
To want to willingly bang my head
They can all fuck off today
I refuse to let them ruin my day
I am determined to get things done
The October sun is good for my bones
I'll wear my long black coat for my walk
Abundantly, absorb the sun's rays
Deliciously warming up my back
Oh, how brilliant that I chose to feel good today
I commend myself for not allowing the voices get their way
Thank you God for being with me always.

Metamorphosis

We are forever changing, growing
Evolving into a newer version
Of self, mind, body, and soul
With no looming shadows
Of our former self
Just like the butterfly, finally
Appearing from its cocoon
After its metamorphic journey
Resurrected into a glorious new form
With its wondrous wings, coloured brightly
Finally ready to take flight
Out of the darkness of its slumber
Into the open skies, so bright
To begin a whole new journey, a whole new life
Caterpillar to butterfly, the highest version of itself.

Shaken Not Stirred

Recently, in my head
I got caught up in a storm
Oblivious of where the raging winds
Were taking me
Would I even make it through
The darkness and the turmoil
Well, here I am, still standing stubbornly
Firmly rooted, in my soul to the earth
Like the trees, just a little shaken
Having shed my summer leaves
I stand naked to grow afresh
With the coming of spring
I am safe
I am me
I am finally home.

Milton Keynes UK
Ingram Content Group UK Ltd.
UKHW020700290424
441924UK00017B/969